Change The Game

Win the Job Interview with the Rule of Three Technique

By Adam Redding

©April 2016 Adam Redding

Table of Contents

Introduction

Thank you for purchasing my interview book - you have taken the first step toward getting your next job! The goal of this book is simple: To help you dramatically increase the probability of landing a job.

How is this book different from others of its ilk? Well, you may have already noticed that the alternatives out there focus on how to answer questions without offering a concrete strategy or framework. The Rule of Three Interview Technique outlined in these pages, on the other hand, provides a framework to answer any interview question. This strategy grapples with the most critical interview topics, such as, "Walk me through your resume," or "Why do you want to work for us?" Rest assured, by sticking to the Rule of Three framework, you will consistently come across as professional, organized, and knowledgeable.

As an added bonus, this technique serves as a tool to buy extra time. Every interview has at least one question that you didn't prepare for. Employing my approach, though, presents you with the time needed to be successful, while not appearing stumped or confused.

Furthermore, too many interview books focus on you, the interviewee. What about the people performing the interview? What are their goals and success metrics? How do you approach the different players? If you want to be successful, you need to understand what the other side thinks. This book walks through the motivations of the key individuals you'll encounter, a strategic advantage when interviewing.

Beyond the above, if you only take away one lesson from this book, it's this: you must change your mentality. For example, if you were running an ecommerce business, you'd want to test different site layouts, consider different messaging, or experiment with different price points. And every time you'd run such a scenario, you'd analyze the results to ascertain what works best, if at all. Only then can you maximize return on investment. Well, guess what – the same works for interviewing! In order to get the most out of this book, you need to commit to being honest with yourself and allow for personal reflection, lesson learning, and improvement.

The different sections of this book

- **Part 1 – Interview Preparation and Tips:** First, I provide a list of preparation tips and principles, as well as things to avoid when interviewing. Then, we'll dig into who's performing the interview so you understand what success metrics they use to evaluate you. With the right mindset and an understanding of the landscape, you'll be ready to start learning strategies for success.

- **Part 2 – The Interview Rule of Three Technique:** I'll provide you with the framework and explain how to use it, why it works, and give concrete examples that aid in constructing your own answers.

This guide is concise, powerful, and it will absolutely help you get your next job.

How to use this guide

This guide should be used in two primary ways:

1. **A step-by-step guide:** This guide offers a framework for interviewing. I recommend that you go in chronological order. In each section, I list next steps that test your skills and put the concepts to use. If you take the time and follow the suggestions in each section, you will get the most value out of this guide.

2. **A reference guide:** This guide can be used at any stage of the interview process. If there are certain questions that you're struggling with, you can easily find suggested responses. That said, I highly recommend going through this book in chronological order and applying the Rule of 3 Technique as it was intended.

A little bit about me, The Author

I have extensive experience on both sides of the interview process. The embarrassing truth is that it once took me more than one hundred interviews at more than forty companies to land a job. I got rejected from eight separate final rounds. Thus my "conversion rate," as defined by jobs landed divided by total interviews, was less than 1%. I was on an emotional rollercoaster! Believe me when I tell you, I get it!

So, why am I writing a book on interviewing? All of the failure forced me to adjust my approach. In doing so, I learned many critical lessons that dramatically changed my success metrics. I have now interviewed hundreds of candidates and examined successful and unsuccessful strategies. From these experiences I honed a framework that is highly successful. And the best part is anyone can use this approach in any industry.

As you'll notice, I have a more analytical bent to interviewing than other coaches. I've worked at large corporations, as well as some of the hottest tech companies in Silicon Valley. I've also written a book on email marketing, "An Introduction to Email Marketing and Strategy", where I apply my analytical approach to marketing. Thus, my hope is that you appreciate this fresh perspective to solving the interview puzzle.

Lastly, on a more personal note, this is my second published book. I sincerely hope you enjoy reading it, and, of course, learn many new things along the way. If you have any feedback, or want to discuss anything further, please email me at authoradamredding@gmail.com. If you feel so inclined, I would greatly appreciate if you'd leave a review on amazon.com once you have finished the book.

Thank you! Now let's build those interview skills!

War Stories

Before we explore the various techniques on how to be a great at interviewing, I want to share two interview war stories. One occurred when I was an interviewee, and the other, when I was the interviewer. The tales will help you get through the dog days of interviewing, when you're feeling the bluest of blues. You'll think to yourself, "Well, I might have embarrassed myself, but not as much as this guy." And maybe, more importantly, they're pretty darn funny. Some humor always helps me pay better attention, which no doubt will assist you here!

My Interview with a Bank

Many years ago, I lived abroad in Hong Kong and was interviewing for jobs so I could relocate back to America. At the time of this particular interview, I was vacationing in Southeast Asia, spending time in Cambodia and Vietnam. This story takes place in a small hotel in Hanoi, which is in northern Vietnam.

I was interviewing for a job at a mid-sized bank located in San Francisco. Back then, I had an itch to get into banking and make the big bucks. After four rounds of interviews, I was scheduled to interview with the CEO. Pretty good, right? But there was a catch: they didn't tell me about the interview until the day before. Since I was on my vacation, I was woefully unprepared.

To make matters worse, the interview was scheduled for 4:30AM Vietnam time, as Vietnam is 15 hours ahead of San Francisco. Figuring out the logistics of a 4:30AM interview in a foreign country where you don't speak the language is no trivial task. I scoured the internet to determine where I could take the phone call; I was traveling with a friend, so unfortunately I didn't have a private room to use as home base. After many failures, I decided that the best place to interview with the CEO was from the bathroom in my hotel room. Yes, that's right, the bathroom. I figured I could close the door and even wake up my roommate!

I arose at 4:00 AM, splashed water on my face, rehearsed a few answers, and took a seat on the toilet (there were no spare chairs), ready to interview. At 4:30AM, I promptly received a call on my cell phone from the CEO. I distinctly remember her saying, "Is it me, or am I hearing echoes from your phone?" Of course, I hadn't realized that in a small room, such as a bathroom, my voice would echo!

I threw open the door and popped the windows, which somewhat helped. She fired question after question. It was challenging to find a rhythm and I fumbled through the answers. As the interview progressed, my back started aching, as I had been sitting on the toilet for almost an hour. I hadn't considered the value of a good chair! Suffice it to say, I was off my game considerably. At the end of the interview, defeated and disheveled, I gazed up to see my roommate standing in front of me with a befuddled look on his face. I can only imagine what he was thinking - his friend, sitting on the toilet with phone in hand and head hung over his shoulders. Defeated.

I never heard back from that company (it's infuriating when that happens!). And the worst part: this was before the days of Skype and the call cost me $100. Talk about kicking someone when they're down!

Many things obviously went wrong during that interview. But most important, I didn't set myself up for success. I had no chance to get the job the moment I sat on that toilet. The right environment and the right mindset are paramount for achieving your goals. Don't underestimate those two factors.

My Interview with a Candidate

This story demonstrates what not to do in an interview. I was meeting a candidate for an analyst position. Early on, I could tell there was something odd about the person. He talked at length about the problems between his mother and father. As the interviewer, I tried to steer the conversation back to the task at hand, but it was futile.

After about 20 minutes, it became clear to the candidate that the interview was not going as planned- I must have given it away with my body language. And that's when things got a bit strange. Here's the exchange:

Interviewee: Do you mind if I open my bag?

Me: Um...well I'm not sure why you would do that. Is everything OK?

Interviewee: No, don't worry. I want to give you something.

Me: Um...OK. I'd really like to keep talking about your candidacy.

At that moment, the interviewee turned around, opened up his bag, and pulled out of all things....a Nerf football. Yes, that's not a typo, a Nerf football! He then asked me if I would take the toy as a gift. Confused and disoriented, I agreed. The interview lasted for five more minutes. Afterwards, I walked over to the HR lead and told him the evaluation process was over for this candidate. I will say, however, that we had the ball in our office for the next year, so that interviewee's gift was thoroughly enjoyed in the end. The moral of the story, you ask? Don't talk about your personal life, and don't give any gifts to the interviewer!

Part 1 – Interview Preparation and Tips

Chapter 1: Committing to the Right Mindset

We've all been there. You made it through the first set of interviews and got the invite to the office for a final round. And after a full day of tireless effort, you've done a great job. But much to your chagrin, you don't immediately hear back from the HR team. You begin to question your answers. With each passing hour, the anxiety worsens. And then, finally, the cell phone rings and you clumsily pick up and learn they went with the other person. You weren't the right fit or didn't have enough experience. Or even worse, they wouldn't even offer a reason, so you're left utterly clueless.

Naturally, that's heartbreaking. You continue thinking about the interview answers, cringing at some of your responses. Your significant other has been nice enough to listen to your complaints, but even he or she tires of your whining and frustration. A few days later, the emotions subside, and you realize it's time to dive back in. It's time to pick yourself up!

These are all natural reactions to the interview process. Frankly, it sucks. But this is typically what happens next: you lock down another interview, go through the same process, emotions swing like a pendulum, and unfortunately, experience the same outcome. You then spiral down again, while trying to figure out what went wrong and becoming despondent; ultimately finding yourself back in the exact same place you were before.

This is what I call the pulse rate. If you look at a heart monitor, it's those up and down zig zags, typically reverting to the mean. This type of behavior implies a healthy person. *But*, in the world of interviewing, this is not a healthy interviewee. Reverting to the mean is a bad thing. We need to breakout, improve, and learn from our mistakes. We need to create step functions. You may be asking, "What's a step function?"

Let's bring back our ecommerce example to explain. You're selling sneakers. And for every 100 visitors to the company website, you sell five sneakers. That's a 5% conversion rate. Not bad! Now, perhaps you change the images of the sneakers and introduce a 360 degrees view. The images have higher resolution and the consumer can see the entire shoe. After introducing that optimization, you start selling 10 sneakers for every 100 visitors. That's a 10% conversion rate, which is twice as high as 5%! The 10% is the new normal. Thus, you've created a step function in your conversion rate. It's illustrated in the graph below.

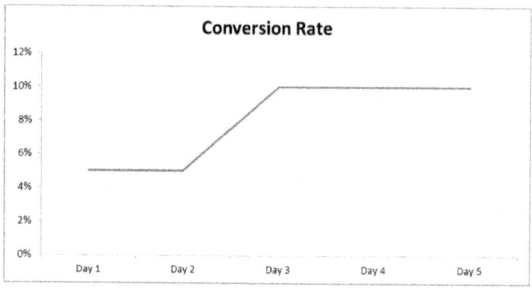

This type of improvement can be translated to interviewing (or anything in life for that matter). You just need to shift your mindset. What do I mean by this? Basically, stop performing and start analyzing.

So, how do you do this? By approaching every interview as an opportunity to learn, that's how. Typically, there are a few minutes between interviews. This is your opportunity to quickly review the previous session and write down notes (bring a notepad or a padfolio to every interview). If you struggled with a question, write that query down during this interim period. Additionally, if you noticed any negative reactions or body motions in response to answers, write them down as well. Lastly, write down the answers to questions that you asked. This is critical. The more you can retain about the position and the team you're interviewing with, the more knowledgeable you will become in every subsequent round.

Once all the interviews are over, review your notes. Take time to understand what worked and what didn't. If you struggled with a question, test out new answers by rehearsing in the mirror or with a friend. With this new approach, you'll quickly become less emotionally involved in the interview process and will naturally start treating it like a learning process, which causes rapid improvement. This is called the growth mindset. With a growth mindset, anything is possible.

Next Steps

In order to begin the process of personal reflection and self-improvement, it's necessary to answer a few questions. Please be honest with yourself. List three to five items for each.

- During the interview process, what have I historically done well?

- What have I struggled with during the interview process?

- What's the strongest part of my resume?

- What's the weakest part of my resume?

Chapter 2: 9 Tips for Interview Preparation

1. **Research** – Read everything about the company you're interviewing with. We'll cover this more in the interview principles section.

2. **Dress to impress** – In my expert opinion, dress conservatively and iron your clothes. Always overdress unless told specifically what to wear by the hiring manager or HR contact.

3. **LinkedIn research** – Research the people you're interviewing with. Don't come off as creepy, but the more you know, the more curveballs you're ready to face. If you know people at the company, reach out to them and ask for advice. This is a perfectly acceptable interview tactic. In fact, it shows how much you want the job.

4. **Go to Glassdoor.com** – This site is an incredible tool to learn potential interview questions. You can also get some insight about company culture and its direction. This is a great place to find inspiration for questions for your interviewers.

5. **Have a list of at least 10 questions for your interviewer** – That's not a typo. There's a chance you get an interviewer who won't ask you any questions. Rather, he or she will sit there and want you to lead the exchange. This is always nerve-racking, so definitely over prepare. And remember to listen to the answers. Turn your mindset from reactionary to curious. If you're inquisitive about the interviewer's responses, you will naturally think of more questions on the

spot. Another tactic is to ask follow up questions. This provides yet another opportunity to learn even more about the position. I'll cover the topic in more detail during the Three Pillars chapter.

6. **Practice in front of the mirror** – This is a classic interview preparation technique. The tactic allows you to hear your responses out loud. Make sure to sound confident. Lean in when answering questions. Pay attention to your eye contact and hand motions. Keep your hand motions within your shoulders and close to the table. If the interviewer notices your hands, immediately place and fold them so they don't move. Lastly, listen for verbal pauses, such as "um," "like," and "you know." It's hard to prevent those words from slipping out, especially when asked something you're unprepared for, but they don't sound professional. Instead, just slow down and take your time. It's fine to wait a few seconds to think about an answer.

7. **Power pose** – When you're sitting in your car before the interview, put your arms above your head. This is the "power pose." It stimulates higher levels of testosterone and lowers that of cortisone, leading to both greater feelings of power and tolerance of risk. Watch the TED video from Amy Cuddy on this subject.

8. **Be early** – Don't ever be late for an interview; it reeks of unprofessionalism. I recommend finding a coffee shop close to the interview's location and getting there 30 minutes prior to the appointed time. Grab a coffee. Use the toilet. Get your head in the right place.

9. **Get excited about the job** – I know this one is often tough. Sometimes, you just want a paycheck. Here's the truth, though: hiring managers want someone excited about the job and the company. If this doesn't come natural to you, practice! Use summary statements (I'll explain later) like, "I'm really excited about this position" or "I'm extremely interested in this company." Read about the company and find things that engage you. Maybe it's not the job itself, but it's something else related to the company. Bring that into the interview so that you appear naturally exuberant.

Next Steps

Pick two of the tips described above and try them before your next interview. Afterwards, write down what worked and what didn't.

Chapter 3: The 5 Job Interviewing Principles That Will Immediately Improve Your Performance

There are five principles to keep in mind while interviewing.

1. **It's a sales pitch** – The interview is not a time to be timid. You are selling yourself. Count on the fact that multiple candidates are being considered for the position. Don't be afraid to be aggressive. Don't be afraid to be sales-y. Every question is an opportunity to sell yourself as the perfect fit for the job. I know many of you are thinking: "I don't want to come off as conceited or pretentious" or "It's hard to be sales-y. It doesn't come natural to me." Those thoughts are natural, but ignore them. Remember, this is a competition and there's only one winner. Practice in the mirror. Practice with friends. Be the salesperson. Boast about accomplishments. Just remember that you do need to be humble. With your growth mindset and personal reflections, you can exude your best self!

2. **Don't make assumptions. You must connect the dots** – Never, and I mean NEVER, assume that the interviewer will connect the dots for you. It will not happen, no matter the subject. YOU must do it for him or her. And you must do it for each person who questions you. Do not assume they talk to each other about specific answers. This is especially critical when told to go through your resume or explain why you're a fit for the role. I'll demonstrate with an example.

Let's say that in your previous job, you worked as a financial analyst for Microsoft. In that role, you made recommendations to internal stakeholders on how to allocate their budget. Now, let's assume that you're interviewing for a life insurance salesperson position with MetLife. Inevitably, you will be asked about your sales skills, because you don't have any obvious sales experience. A typical question and answer might go like this:

Interviewer: Why do you think you can excel in life insurance sales when you have no previous sales experience?

Interviewee: Great question. In my opinion, I have very good sales skills. In my previous role, one of my key functions was to advise internal stakeholders on how to allocate their budget. For example, when I worked with the Xbox team, I weighed in on how to finance the production of the Xbox controllers. The Xbox team came to me with three options for financing. After running the analysis and assessing all alternatives, I shared my recommendations. In the presentation, I used data to prove that financing the production of the controllers through a term loan was the most cost effective way of proceeding. I outlined the costs and benefits of each alternative and summarized my findings for the entire ream. The result was that they emphatically agreed, and this decision saved the company $10 million. My sales skills were crucial to convincing the Xbox team to move forward with my conclusions.

On the surface, this is an impressive response. The candidate did a great job describing why he has great analytical and presentation skills. By all accounts, he's a good salesman as well. However, the problem is that while he proves he has sales skills, he doesn't connect that to why he would be a good life insurance salesman. Just having impressive sales skills isn't good enough. A better answer would be to finish with the following.

Interviewee: ...The result was that they emphatically agreed, and this decision saved the company $10 million. Now, I know I have never sold life insurance, and if given the opportunity I will certainly need to learn the ins and outs of life insurance products. That said, I would imagine that to be a great life insurance salesman, you need strong interpersonal skills, you must communicate very well, and you will need to explain complex products to often uneducated clients. My ability to concisely and clearly explain intricate financial products to non-financial experts, coupled with strong presentation and sales skills, as evidenced by this example, will allow me to be a highly effective life insurance salesman.

See the difference? In the second example, you connected the dots in a concise and intelligent manner. You also appeared humble by acknowledging the fact that you don't have experience in the field, which is another great interview tactic.

3. **You're in control** – Do not forget this. The interviewers are going to ask questions to uncover holes in your story. They're going to throw curveballs to catch you off guard. It's critical that you remember that you control your words. Take your time and think about your answers. Carefully navigate questions to focus on your strengths, while steering the conversation away from your weaknesses. This builds off the growth mindset we discussed earlier. The more you practice, the easier it will get. And this is critical for the next principle.

4. **Minimize risk** – If there are weaknesses in your resume, don't bring them up. If the interviewer asks about a sore spot, then surely address it directly. But when in doubt, always direct the conversation to your strengths. Don't go off on tangents and don't ramble. Stick to the script and stick to your strengths. Shorter answers are better than longer answers because long answers offer your inquisitor more opportunities to probe. If you don't immediately have an answer, it's fine to ask the interviewer to repeat the question or ask it another way. Do whatever you can to buy extra time so you can think up a concise, effective answer.

5. **Over prepare** – I have many mottos in life, but the following is key: failing to prepare is preparing to fail. Here are examples for how to prepare for an interview:

- If you're interviewing at a public company, read the 10K, know the stock price, and read the latest public announcements.

- Know the name of the CEO. If he or she has a book, buy it and read the first chapter.

- If the company has a consumer facing product, use it. I cannot tell you how many times I ask candidates about our product and they have never used it.

- Go to LinkedIn and see if you're connected with anyone at the company. If so, try to set up a call with them to learn more.

- If you are part of an alumni network, see if there are any alumni that work at the company. Then try to set up a call with them. The closer to your potential position, the better.

Chapter 4: The 10 Job Interview Tips for What Not To Do

Here's a list of things to avoid. These items, of course, are not exhaustive, but relevant nonetheless.

1. **Don't ramble** – I mention this in the minimizing risk section. If you start rambling, it implies you don't know what you're talking about. It also typically leads to saying something about a weakness.

2. **Don't talk about your personal life** – There are times when it could be appropriate, but generally speaking, keep your personal life out of it. I have had interviewees discuss their parents' divorce, various childhood dramas, and bad breakups, amongst other topics. In most contexts, it's awkward. And again, don't give the interviewer the opportunity to think you're weird. Minimize your risk.

3. **Don't use excessive hand motions** – Keep your hands within your shoulders, either on the table or on your lap. Feel free to use small hand motions, but keep it to just that. If the interviewer starts noticing your hands, reduce your hand motions immediately.

4. **Don't badmouth previous companies** – It does not reflect well on you to talk negatively about companies on your resume. It's natural to have a few bad experiences, but be sure to paint them in the right light. If you talk negatively about a previous company, it implies that you will talk negatively about the company you're interviewing for now in the future. I've seen CEO's reject candidates at the last minute because of this.

5. **Don't come underdressed** – This is a sensitive one. It's hard to know exactly what to wear. Unless given specific instructions by the recruiter or a key contact at the company, overdress (as I mentioned earlier). Overdressing typically means wearing a suit. Use your judgment, of course but always lean toward overdressing.

6. **Don't follow up post interview with answers to questions you got wrong** – If you think you answered a question incorrectly, do not follow up with an answer. Nothing good ever comes from that approach. If you feel that one question was the determining factor in your candidacy, you're wrong. And if you think that answering that question after the fact will help you, you are dead wrong. Swallow your pride, wait to hear back, and then learn from your mistakes using the growth mindset.

I'll tell you a story that demonstrates the above error. Many years ago, I worked on a trading floor at a major investment bank. During an interview, a hiring manager asked a complicated math question. After spending five minutes trying to solve the problem, the candidate failed and was sent home. The interviewee then proceeded to write the hiring manger a two page email explaining how to solve the math problem. Now, how do I know about all this? Well, upon receiving the message, the hiring manager printed it out, stood on his chair, and read the contents to more than one hundred people on the trading floor. Everyone laughed until they cried. Personally, I thought the behavior was despicable; it's one of the reasons I changed careers. But, we live in a world where such actions are not atypical, so don't let this happen to you. . Mistakes happen, but the key is to learn from them, not exacerbate them.

7. **Don't curse** – Please watch your language. Cursing implies that you don't communicate professionally in the workplace.

8. **When asked if you have questions, don't say no** – Always prepare questions. Asking questions implies that you're curious, which is a critical skill for a successful employee. Always ask at least three questions. It's unlikely that your many interviewers will talk to each other, so don't worry

about repeating questions with each of them. But if you prepare 10 questions, like I suggested earlier, you should be able to easily ask different questions to each person.

9. **Don't pull out a smartphone or a tablet** – Imagine an interview where a candidate opens his or her iPad to read pre-written answers to questions. This is a true story, it happened to me. Do not look at your phone or use technology during your interview.

10. **Don't appear arrogant** – There's a fine line between boasting about your accomplishments and appearing arrogant. Always credit your team and your colleagues for success while focusing on how your accomplishments improved the company's top and bottom lines.

Chapter 5: The Cast of Characters

In order to win the interview, you need to understand the goals and motivations of the people on the other side of the table. Those desires are going to significantly change, though, depending on the job. For example, a college student interviewing for his or her first job at a bank will have a dramatically different experience than a person seeking a manufacturing job at General Motors. That said, there are generally a few characters that stay consistent throughout the process. Let's dissect them.

The Recruiter

The recruiter typically sits on the HR team. This person is responsible for finding the best possible candidates for the job. He or she is often compensated by how many candidates are hired, so they want to make sure the people they recommend to hiring managers are great fits. They want you to succeed, because if you succeed, they succeed. Let's go through the three stages of the hiring process:

1. **Vetting** – A good recruiter should have vetted you before setting up a call. They want to make sure you're as good as your resume indicates. You can expect to hear, "Walk me through your resume" and "Why this company?" Your job is to appear knowledgeable, eager, and smart. If you reach this point, you're already in a good position. The truth is, the goal is to not say something stupid. If you can minimize that risk, you're ahead of the game.

2. **Support** – Once the recruiter vets you and decides you're a good fit, he'll be on your side because he is incentivized to see you succeed. Thus, asking the recruiter questions about next steps can be helpful. You should be extremely curious because the more you can learn, the better prepared you will be. The recruiter becomes your friend during this stage.

3. **Negotiation** – If you've made it this far, then fantastic. The recruiter will typically be the voice of the hiring manager as it relates to negotiation. I can write an entire book on negotiation, so I'll leave it there for now.

Hiring Manager

The hiring manager is the most important player in this game. He or she is the person that will make the ultimate decision because that's who you'll probably work for. This person's motivation is to find the best person for the job. They want to be assured that you're the right fit. They like relevant experience, which minimizes the risk of a bad hire. If the hire goes south, they want to be able to point their boss to those obvious qualifications so they don't get fired for the mistake.

What's most important to the hiring manager?

- Relevant experience

- Proper skillset

- Work ethic

- Intelligence

- Professionalism

- Personality/fit

Now that you understand what the hiring manager cares about, you need to articulate your responses to convey the above criteria.

The Executive

In most interviews, you will eventually interview with the hiring manager's boss. I call this person the executive. He or she is there to support the hiring manager and help guarantee that the candidate is a good fit for the role. This player is typically looking for the following:

- Holes in the resume

- Areas of weakness

- Personality/fit

- Knowledge about the company

- Attitude/motivations

- Career goals

Next steps

For your next interview, write down the key players and match them to the recruiter, hiring manager and executive. Then, take the job description and everything you know about the position and list three skills that each player desires. Once you have the list, come up with two examples that demonstrate those skillsets. Don't worry, it's likely that there will be overlapping examples and skills.

Part Two - The Interview Rule of Three Technique

Chapter 6: Situation Action Result

Thus far, you have learned about the growth mindset, been educated on interview dos and don'ts, and met the cast of characters. It's now time to introduce the Rule of Three Technique. I'm going to start with Situation Action Result, which is the backbone of the strategy.

Situation Action Result is a classic interview tool to use when using an example to answer a question. I find this approach incredibly useful with behavioral questions. This tactic fits directly into the Rule of Three Technique, which I will explain in the next chapter. For those of you already familiar with this strategy, please note that I have combined "Task" with "Situation," since I believe these can both be accomplished at the same time.

What are behavioral questions? They are queries that assess the candidate's previous work experience, and based on that knowledge, imply how the candidate will perform in similar situations.

Explanation

Situation – When asked a question, the first thing you want to do is explain the situation, provide context, and describe the challenge. You want to mention when and where this event took place. You want to illuminate what needed to be done.

Action – Talk specifically about what actions you took to solve the problem. What tools did you use? How did you interact with other team members? How did you use data and analytics to solve the problem?

Result – Explain the results of solving the problem. Quantitatively and qualitatively, what happened? Discuss the specific benefits to the business, as well as the overall impact on yourself and the team.

Example

Task –

Describe a situation when you used persuasion to successfully convince someone to see things your way.

Answer –

Situation: As a product manager, one of my key responsibilities is to come up with solutions to optimize our website. I had a great idea for a test that I felt would dramatically improve our revenue. Unfortunately, we have limited developer resources, so in order to launch the test, I needed to convince my boss that it was worth running.

Action: I did three things to ensure he couldn't say no. One, I put together a business case explaining the cost of developer time vs. the expected impact to revenue. Secondly, I organized the case into an executive summary so that my boss could easily interpret my analysis, as well as pass that summary around internally. Lastly, I organized a meeting with him and the other stakeholders to ensure that all the right people were in the room. I then presented my executive summary to the team.

Result – The result was that my boss and the rest of the team agreed to run the test. The results showed a 35% improvement in our conversion rate, which led to a $100K increase in revenue. By preparing a thorough analysis and ensuring the key decision makers were in the room, I was able to convince the team to run a test that dramatically increased our revenue.

The above statement is concise, organized, and directly answers the question. It sets up the scene, discusses the tasks used for persuasion, and then details the impact on the business. Lastly, and often forgotten, the interviewee summarizes the entire response in one statement that highlights key qualities that will be important to the job (preparation, analysis, communication, persuasion).

As you can see above, this structure is set up in three stages. This makes it easy for you to remember, especially when given a question that you were unprepared for. I'll dive deeper into this structure in the next chapter.

Next Steps

Prepare your own version of the above example, using the Situation Action Result framework.

Chapter 7: Interview Technique Part 1 – The Rule of Three

It seems like all things in life come in threes. There are The Three Musketeers, The Three Stooges, the three little pigs, the three French hens, three strikes in a baseball game, and of course the Lord of the Rings trilogy (the Hobbit was a great book, but don't talk to me about the movies). I am also one of three brothers. Three is good! So, it shouldn't be surprising there's a Rule of Three when it comes to interviewing.

As it relates to interviewing, the Rule of Three is powerful. In writing, there's a concept called "the Power of Three." This conceit suggests that things that come in three are easier to understand, which makes the audience more likely to remember what was said. That's because this structure combines brevity and rhythm. One of the reasons the characters listed above have stayed so prominent in our culture is because they are easy to remember. And this is incredibly important. The interviewer needs to easily understand what you're saying. If you don't connect your thoughts coherently, you won't be memorable (at least, in the positive way you'd want to be recalled). Thus, you need to make it incredibly easy for the interviewer to understand why you're the perfect fit for the job.

So, how does the Rule of Three work? The strategy is defined by structure. When applicable, your answers should be set up in a three tiered framework that is separated by transitions. Your response should be delivered using the following language:

- First....

- Secondly, or next, or additionally….

- Third, or lastly, or finally, or as a final point….

Next, when using the transition words above, connect them with a direct answer to the question. For example, "First, I want to work at Google because Google is the most innovative company in the world." The response is concise and directly answers a question.

Simple, right? This works incredibly well for requests and questions like:

- Walk me through your resume

- Why do you want to work at this company?

- Why do you want to be in this industry?

- Where do you see yourself in five years?

- Why should I hire you?

- What are your greatest strengths?

- What are your greatest weaknesses?

- What motivates you?

Let's evaluate two examples for this question: why do you want to work for Google?

Example 1 – Without the Rule of Three

I want to work for Google because Google is the most innovative company in the world. Not only does Google provide the world's best search engine, but Google's product velocity is incredible. They've been able to release so many influential products, such as Chromecast, Wi-Fi hot air balloons, Google Glass, and even self-driving cars. Also I've talked to many people and the culture is fantastic. From what I understand, Google fosters a collaborative environment as well as provides many amenities that make working at Google a great experience. Google also has a world-class management team. When joining a company, it's critical to believe in the management's vision for the company. Larry and Sergei are two of the brightest executives in the world and it would be an incredible opportunity to help them and the rest of the Google team continue to march forward.

Generally speaking, this isn't bad. But let's take a look using the Rule of Three Technique.

Example 2 – Using the Rule of Three

There are three reasons why I want to work at Google. First, Google is the most innovative company in the world. Not only does Google provide the world's best search engine, but the product velocity is incredible. They've been able to release so many influential products, such as Chromecast, Wi-Fi hot air balloons, Google Glass, and even self-driving cars. Secondly, the culture is fantastic. From what I understand, Google fosters a collaborative environment as well as provides many amenities that make working at Google a great experience. Lastly, Google has a world-class management team. When joining a company, it's critical to believe in the management vision for the company. Larry and Sergei are two of the brightest executives in the world and it would be an incredible opportunity to help them and the rest of the Google team continue to march forward.

Let's examine the differences:

- "There are three reasons why I want to work at Google"– This is a powerful statement. It's direct, implying that you're confident about your answer. Secondly, and most importantly, it indicates to the interviewer that he or she should look for three topics. I cannot emphasize this enough. By tipping them off, they're dramatically more likely to remember your responses.

- Structure – The Rule of Three approach allows you to directly answer the question, and then gives you a framework to support your answer. Each time you use the First, Second or Lastly cue, you alert the interviewer that you are about to offer a direct answer. Thus, the interviewer is more likely to listen when those words are used. Let's examine those sentences:

  - First, Google is the most innovative company in the world.

  - Secondly, the culture is fantastic.

  - Lastly, Google has a world-class management team.

Simple, concise, powerful, and easy to remember. This structure can be applied to almost any question. Why not take a look at a question that's more challenging?

Question: Do you handle conflict well?

Rule of Three Answer

Yes, I believe I handle conflict very well. Historically when I've had to deal with conflict, I've tackled it in three ways:

First, I would reach out to the colleague directly and have a professional conversation about the problem. I've found this to be the most effective approach. For example, I once had a colleague that got so angry over a disagreement that he stopped speaking to me (situation). In order to convince him to chat, I offered to buy him a coffee. He initially refused, but with some old fashioned persistence, he relented. I directly confronted him about the disagreement, apologized if he misinterpreted my point of view, and offered him the opportunity to discuss his thoughts (action). The result was that he apologized. In fact, he felt so badly about the situation that he helped me push through a couple of initiatives that had been stalled (result).

Secondly, if I'm unable to convince my colleague to speak, I would reach out to a peer to inquire on my behalf. I would use this approach only if I'm unable to have a conversation directly. This is often better than going to a boss because the last thing I want to do is get someone in hot water with a manager. I find that this works most of the time.

Lastly, if I'm unable to solve the issue using the previous two tactics, I would have my manager set up a conversation with his or her manager, and then the four of us could meet together. This way, it doesn't look like I went directly over anyone's head since my manager initiated the conversation. Ultimately, the key to solving conflict is to have a direct conversation. By using the three tactics I just described, I've been able to successfully navigate all work conflicts that I've encountered.

The Rule of Three approach clearly articulates three approaches to resolving conflict. In each section, begin with one sentence that directly answers the question. This way the interviewer can easily write down your answer. Then support that response with one or two sentences. I suggest using an example for one of the three responses and keeping the answer to 1 – 2 minutes. Last, finish with a summary statement that emphatically answers the original question.

Next Steps

Pick a company that you're interviewing with and brainstorm three reasons why you want to work there. Then, using those reasons, write your explanation using the Rule of Three Technique. Keep tweaking the answer until it sounds right.

Chapter 8: Interview Technique Part 2 – The Three Pillars

The second part of the Rule of Three Interview Technique focuses on the three most important areas of the interview:

- The first five minutes

- The Pitch

- Asking questions

The first five minutes

I cannot emphasize this enough – **first impressions matter!** The first five minutes are critical for steering the remainder of the interview. Your contact will make a decision about you quickly. According to qz.com, 30% of interviewers will decide in the first five minutes whether they like you. Once you get to 15 minutes, that number is close to 70%. Thus, it's crucial to make a great first impression.

There's no guarantee what subjects will come up in the first 5 minutes. However, most interviews will open with "Walk me through your resume" or "Tell me about yourself." This is your opportunity to sell yourself and explain why you're the perfect fit for the position.

How to answer "Walk me through your resume"

Tell a story that connects the dots: Your goal is to tell the interviewer exactly why you're the perfect fit for the position based on your previous work history. Key items to include:

- **Theme:** What is your theme for wanting the job and why are you a great fit? You should have 2 – 3 underlying reasons why you want the job. Your story should reinforce those reasons as often as possible. For example, I want to work as an industry analyst at an automotive company. My themes are: I'm a great analyst, I have a strong understanding of the automotive market, and I have highly relevant experience. Your story should support that theme.

- **A brief history of your past two to three jobs**. You want to briefly talk about the 1 or 2 things you did at each job that's most relevant to the current job. Use your theme above to connect the jobs together.

- **Connections**. You must connect each job. Why did you leave Company A and go to work at Company B? How does that support your theme as to why you are a great fit for the job?

- **A description of 1-3 skills that you learned at each job.** These skills should be directly correlated to the position you're interviewing for. Examples include: Analytics, communication, presenting, persuasion, computer programming, relationship building, patience, management, listening, innovation, organization, project management, etc.

- **Sales pitch:** As you're noticing, selling is a big part of my strategy. After you tell your story, summarize exactly why you're a great fit for the position. This is your summary statement, which allows the interviewer to remember one statement as to why you're ideal for the job.

Example – Interviewing for an Industry Analyst position at an automotive company

Interviewer: Hi Adam. Walk me through your resume. What should I know about you?

Adam: Of course. Three years ago I worked as an analyst at General Motors. I was responsible for aggregating the data that we used in our analyst reports and then running the forecast to predict where the market was heading. For example, when we released our annual forecast numbers, I was responsible for:

- One - Collecting the data. I aggregated data from more than 20 sources.

- I then used a proprietary forecast tool I built to predict the performance of the automotive market.

- Lastly, I presented this data to the lead analyst and she used it in her interviews with the media.

- This helped me develop strong analytical skills, as well as hone my presentation capabilities that will be critical for this position. I was promoted a year early for my hard work and ability to learn quickly.

- While at GM, I fell in love with the auto industry and the data that goes into understanding what makes the market tick. For my next job, I wanted to further delve into the nuts and bolts of the dealership market because I aimed to become even more competent about the overall industry.

Thus, for my next position, I took an offer at AutoWorld, the largest dealership group in the country, where I have been for the past two years. My responsibility is to optimize our vehicle inventory so we can maximize our sales and profitability. During the last two years, I have further developed my analytical skills, while also improving my ability to spot trends and changes in the data that are critical to predicting future outcomes. Additionally, for the first time, I was interviewed by multiple media sources to discuss my understanding of dealership inventory and how that affects profitability. This experience allowed me to hone my media interviewing skills.

For my next job, I want to be in a position where I can take what I have learned and apply it as a general industry analyst, since I now have a full understanding of the two most important sides of the automotive market. This job opportunity fits my career goals perfectly. Also, over the past three years, I have dramatically improved my ability to analyze both market trends and dealership and manufacturer profitability, as well as forecast the future of the automotive market. I have done this while working at the largest automotive manufacturer in America, as well as the largest dealership group in the country. I'm confident that I have the experience, skillset, and industry expertise to be an incredible industry analyst at your company. I'm excited about the opportunity and I'm eager to get involved.

Let's break down this response for key success metrics:

- **Theme:** The theme in the above: I'm a great analyst, I have a strong understanding of the automotive market, and I have highly relevant experience.

- **A brief history of your past two to three jobs:** I talk about my role at General Motors and AutoWorld, two companies that are in the automotive industry. You need to explain your jobs and why they tie directly to the job you're seeking.

- **Connections:** Let's analyze the connectors:

  o After your first job: "For my next job, I wanted to further delve into the nuts and bolts of the dealership market because I aimed to become even more competent about the overall industry."

  o Second job, first sentence: "Thus, for my next position, I took an offer at AutoWorld, the largest dealership group in the country, where I have been for the past two years." The use of the word "Thus" is a strong connector word, as it clearly attaches the previous work experience to the next.

  o Job you're interviewing for: "For my next job, I want to be in a position where I can take what I have learned and apply it as a general industry analyst, since I now have a full understanding of the two most important sides of the automotive market." This now connects my first two experiences to what I'm looking for next, which is exactly the job I'm interviewing for.

- **A description of 1-3 skills that you learned at each job.** It's always best to be direct in interviews. I discussed analytical skills, presentation skills, and data skills.

- **Sales pitch:** Lastly, I finished the interview with a summary of why I'm a great fit for this job. I also added that I think this is a great opportunity and that I'm very excited about the role: "This job opportunity fits my career goals perfectly. Also, over the past three years, I have dramatically improved my ability to analyze both market trends and dealership and manufacturer profitability, as well as forecast the future of the automotive market. I have done this while working at the largest automotive manufacturer in America, as we ll as the largest dealership group in the country. I'm confident that I have the experience, skillset, and industry expertise to be an incredible analyst at your company. I'm excited about the opportunity and I'm eager to get involved."

Next Steps

Redo your "Walk me through your resume" using the above approach. Make sure to tailor your response to a specific company.

The Pitch

The concept of "The Pitch" is a powerful interview tool, but it needs to be used with the right person at the opportune time or it can backfire. An interview is typically structured as a list of questions asked by the interviewer, followed by an opportunity for the interviewee to ask questions. Let's call this shift the "Question Transition." The "Question Transition" presents an opportunity to take control of the conversation. Here's how it all works:

Directly before the "Question Transition", take a brief moment to pitch the interviewer exactly why you're the best fit for the position. Now, this move is unorthodox and is meant to catch the interviewer by surprise, but I've used it several times when interviewing for positions with great success. Why does this work?

1. **It's unusual** – This will surprise the interviewer. It's not unprofessional or inappropriate. Rather, it demonstrates your passion and desire for the position. You immediately differentiate yourself from the competition.

2. **It allows you to reiterate your skills** – As I have mentioned numerous times, it's critical that the interviewer remembers the key reasons why you want the job. This gives you one final opportunity to control the conversation and ensure the interviewer does not forget why you're the perfect fit for the position.

3. **It shows you want it** – You need to show you want it, that you'll go above and beyond. With this approach, everything is on the table. It's a risk, but in the best possible way. And I can guarantee that no other candidate will be doing this.

When to use it

The technique should be used primarily with the hiring manager. This is the most important person on the other side of the table. He or she needs to hear how much you want the job. They need to feel your passion. Here are my guidelines:

- Use this a maximum of two times during the interview process, definitely with the hiring manager

- Other targets: The executive senior people on the team.

- Do not use the technique with a junior interviewer.

- If you've been recruited for the position, do not use it.

- If you're an executive or interviewing for an executive position, do not use it.

- Be passionate and direct.

- Reiterate your most relatable skills

Example

Interviewer: Do you have any questions for me?

Interviewee: Yes, I have a few. However, before I dive into my questions, if you don't mind, I'd like to summarize why I think I'm a great fit for this position. In order to be successful in this role, you need to have world class analytical, communication, and presentation skills, and the ability to think creatively when there are rapid changes in the marketplace. Given my similar experience at GM and AutoWorld, I strongly believe that I have built those skills over the past three years and would be an ideal fit for the job. Moreover, and most importantly, I believe in the future and vision of this company. I'm eager to be a part of what's happening here and I feel I can be a great asset to this organization. I hope you strongly consider me for the position.

That's a direct and powerful statement. You clearly demonstrate your knowledge of the position, why you think you can be successful, why you want to be a part of this company, and ultimately, your desire and passion for the role.

If you're struggling to get a job, or feeling overly ambitious, you should consider adding the following:

Lastly, you're most likely interviewing many candidates. I'm sure they are all very qualified. I will tell you that I will work harder, stay longer, and be more productive than any of them. I'm eager to dive in and start producing for you and the company immediately.

This is a very direct, aggressive approach. I only recommend using it if you've been out of work for some time and you're having issues finding a job because it could potentially backfire.

Next steps

Create your own pitch. Take some time to think about why you really want the job. You need to find what makes you passionate or interested in this company. Then use that in your pitch to come off as genuine and eager.

Asking questions

Asking thought provoking questions is a critical skill when trying to land a job. It implies curiosity and the more curious the interviewee, the more he or she will learn about the business and processes. And it's these people who ultimately suggest ways to improve the business. Suffice it to say, this is your opportunity to prove how curious you are. It's also a chance to demonstrate how prepared you are, in addition to how well you listened during the interview process. Remember, everything you learn throughout the entire interview process should be repurposed for your benefit.

How do you ask good questions?

Here are three ways to ensure you ask great questions:

1. **Over prepare:** As I stated earlier in this book, failing to prepare is preparing to fail. I highly recommend you think up ten questions prior to the interview. The key is to ask questions that you can use to uncover information that help land the job. Here's a list of standard questions that are good to use.

   Questions to learn more about the role so you can better describe why you're the right fit for this job

   - What are the keys to success in this job?

   - What are the most important skills to be successful in this job?

   - What is the typical day for someone in this role?

   - What are some of the challenges that your team faces?

   - If anyone has failed at this job, why did they fail?

   - What concerns do you have about my candidacy?

Questions about the department so you can understand where you fit within the organization

- How is your department structured?

- How do you interact with other departments within the organization?

- Which departments are most important to your team's success?

- What are your department goals?

- What are the success metrics for your department?

Questions to learn more about the company so you can speak more intelligently about the organization

- What are the biggest challenges facing your company?

- What has your company done well in the last year?

- What are the company goals during the coming year?

- What defines a successful year for the company?

2. **Be curious:** Nothing can replace being prepared. However, there's a finite number of questions to ask and it's not unusual to forget some due to the pressure of the situation. So, how can we solve this? Be curious! This is challenging for many people. How often do you find yourself thinking so hard about asking a question that you forget to listen to what the other person is saying? It's quite common so don't feel badly if this happens to you.

When you're speaking with friends and family, you're genuinely interested in what they have to say. You probably find yourself asking questions all the time. Well, we need to replicate that mindset! In order to do that, we have to become better listeners. If you're listening and paying attention, questions will naturally come to mind. The best questions are asked as a result of what the interviewer is saying. If you can become a better listener, you will become better at asking questions. Here are some listening tips:

- Make eye contact and nod your head when the interviewer is speaking

- Lean forward in your chair

- Smile and use other facial expressions at appropriate times

- Use brief affirmations such as "mrm-hrm," "uh huh," or "yes"

- Summarize the interviewer points after he or she finishes speaking. For example, start off by saying "What I'm hearing is" or "Sounds like you are saying" or "So what you're saying is".

- If a question comes to mind, or you have an idea, write it down. Then continue listening. Don't try to jump in and talk.

- Similarly, if the interviewer says something interesting, write it down. This helps reinforce the concept.

- Do not: Cross your arms, fidget, lose eye contact, interrupt, day dream

3. **The Two Whys:** There's a concept advocated by mindtools.com positing that in order to get to the root cause of a problem, you need to ask why five times. They call this the "Five Whys Rule," which is a probing technique to learn more about a particular problem. This strategy can be applied to interviewing, since our goal is to learn more about the company, the position, the department, and virtually anything that can help us land the job. However, as opposed to five whys, I suggest going with two whys, because anything more might irritate the interviewer. I'll demonstrate with two examples.

Question: What are some of the challenges facing your team?

Response: Our team has struggled to get the necessary resources to grow our business. If we're going to hit our revenue targets this year, we will need to rely more on other departments.

Unfortunately, we've had a tight budget this year since our growth has slowed. That said, there's light at the end of the tunnel so those resources are coming.

Question: Why have you struggled to get resources?

Response: Well, management has had to make some tough resource allocation decisions this year as our growth has slowed. We've been investing in new revenue opportunities as our core business has seen a significant slowdown.

Question: Interesting. Why do you think the core business has slowed down this year?

Response: That's a great question. I think it's market saturation. We've been marketing our product on television, radio and digital for more than two years now. At some point, most consumers have seen your product. It's now time to figure out new ways to grow our business.

Conclusion: Understood. Thank you for that detailed explanation. On a different topic, what do you think are the keys to success in this particular role?

We could of course go on, but I think you get the point. This framework gives you a strategy for listening to the interviewer responses and coming up with ways to ask follow up questions.

Next Steps

Prepare a list of ten questions for your interview. You can use the questions above, if you would like. However, make sure that three of the questions are specific to the company. You can accomplish this by researching the company and coming up with questions based on what you learn.

Chapter 9: Follow-up Email

This chapter is short because the follow-up email is overhyped. I have never seen a job won because of it. On the contrary, I have seen jobs lost due to messing it up. It's arguably an unnecessary part of the process. However, some companies will expect it, so you should always write one. The email should be brief. Never, and I mean never, share anything in the email that can hurt you. It should always be innocuous. Here's my proposed structure:

- Thank the interviewer for his or her time

- Briefly discuss your conversation in a polite and non-specific manner

- Finish by telling the interviewer that you're looking forward to next steps

Hi Timothy,

Thank you for your time yesterday. It was great having the chance to speak with you and learn more about the role and the company. I look forward to hearing back on next steps.

Best regards,

Adam

Lastly, if you interviewed with multiple people, do not be concerned about sending the same email to all of them (though don't forget to change the name!). Nine times out of ten, the interviewers are going to delete the emails. The only time I would be concerned is if you're interviewing as part of a "super day." Many banks, consulting companies, and CPG companies have them. In this case, I would slightly change the thank you note for each interviewer. Generally speaking, though, do not spend a lot of time on the email, and do not stress this part of the interview process.

Next Steps

Using the above template, write a follow-up email example and keep it handy for your next set of interviews.

Chapter 10: Interview Questions and Answers

The following examples will help you craft your interview responses. I'll show you how to answer both general and behavioral questions.

Where do you see yourself in five years?

This is a question that I place in my least favorite bucket. How can you ask me where I'm going to be in five years when I can't see the future? Nevertheless, we need to answer it.

What is the interviewer trying to understand? The interviewer wants to know your career goals and ensure that those goals match the role. Your long-term career goals should parallel the trajectory of the position and the team you'd join. They also want to know that you're not going to leave in six months. Thus answering the question with, "I want to start a company in the near future," is not the best answer.

Some experts will tell you that it's better to answer this question vaguely. My advice, as you can probably guess, is to sell yourself on the position when the opportunity arises.

My approach:

- Propose a clear path of growth related to the position you're interviewing for.

- Provide three reasons why you think you can accomplish those goals (which are really reasons why you're the perfect fit for the position). Use the Rule of Three technique.

- Acknowledge that things can change in the future, which shows humility and self-awareness.

Using the Rule of Three Technique, here's a sample answer for an operations manager position, reporting directly into the Vice President of Operations. The position manages the Los Angeles operation of a ridesharing service.

Example

My long-term goal is to become the Chief Operating Officer of a company. In order to accomplish that goal, over the next five years I would like to grow into a Director and eventually a Vice President of Operations. Things change, of course, but I believe this role and this company are the ideal next step to achieve my short-term and long-term goals. I believe I can accomplish these goals because:

1. First, I love the nature of running a business. My responsibility will be to grow and optimize all areas of the operation. This gets me excited and I have a proven track record doing that at Company 'XYZ'.

2. Secondly, I have a passion for managing people. In this role, it's critical that you have great relationships with your team. This is an area I thrive in and I have extensive experience managing large teams.

3. Lastly, I love analyzing data. In today's marketplace, to be a successful operations manager, data needs to be your best friend, and you have to use it to your advantage. This is an area that I excel in.

With my passion for operations and my relevant skillset, I think I can achieve these goals over the next five years.

Why should I hire you?

This is a great question. You should be praying you're asked this question. It's basically saying – Why are you the person for this job? Sell me on you!

What is the interviewer trying to understand? The interviewer wants to know why you're the perfect fit for this position. Hopefully, you've been listening and asking questions throughout the entire interview process so you know exactly what they're looking for, and what skills are necessary for success. Thus, now is your opportunity to take what you've learned, combined with your strengths and experience, and clearly articulate why you're the PERFECT fit for the job.

My approach:

- Directly acknowledge that you think you're a great fit for the position because of your experience and skillset. It's critical that you include "experience and skillset" because you're backing up your bold statement with concrete evidence. Without the supporting material, you might appear arrogant.

- Provide three reasons why you're the perfect fit for the position. Use the Rule of Three Technique.

- Conclude by briefly summarizing what they're looking for and why you're ideal. This is your summary statement.

Using the Rule of Three Technique, here's a sample answer for the same position as above (operations manager position, reporting directly into the Vice President of Operations. The position manages the Los Angeles operation of a ridesharing service).

Example

Sure! I believe I'm a great fit for this position because of my highly relevant experience, as well as my skillset. I've heard throughout the interview process that in order to be successful in this role, you need to be organized, be great at managing a large team, and execute effectively. I believe I have all of these skills. For example,

1. At Ford Motor Company, I launched a special discount program for recent college grads so they could get extra savings when purchasing a new vehicle. This required me to work with numerous cross functional teams, including the fleet, risk management, finance, operations, legal, and product development teams. I project managed the entire operation, which required exceptional organizational skills as I needed to hit numerous milestones, as well as keep stakeholders on target. This project lasted almost a year, but I'm proud to say that we launched the discount program three months faster than we planned, and this helped drive a five percent improvement in Ford sales over a six-month period. It took strong organizational and project management skills to pull this off, which I know are critical for success in this role.

2. Additionally, I managed a team of five people for more than two years. Over that period, I developed strong managerial skills that have prepared me to lead an even larger team to successfully launch the Los Angeles operation.

3. Lastly, I've always had a reputation as someone who gets things done. Before working at Ford, I was at a small startup in New York City selling popsicles. In this role, I set up the internet business so we could sell directly to consumers. I worked with our front-end and back-end engineers to launch the website. We went from conception to launch in three months. We then doubled our sales over the next three months as we were successful at garnering traffic to the site and converting them into buyers. Once again, my project management skills, my ability to keep a team focused on the big goals, and my strong work ethic were critical to the success we experienced.

As I've learned through this process, organization, management skills and execution are critical for success in this role. Given my experience and skillset, I believe I am the ideal fit for this position.

What are your greatest strengths?

This question is very similar to the prior question, but asked slightly differently. Your job is to focus on the intersection between your skillset and the skillset that the employer desires. The approach used in the "Why Should I Hire You" question is a great example for answering this, with minor tweaks.

What is the interviewer trying to understand? The interviewer wants to know what your strengths are and if they match the company's needs. This is repeating a lot of what we've already discussed.

My approach:

- Use the Rule of Three Technique and focus on three strengths.

- Provide three strengths that perfectly align with the role.

- Finish by saying these strengths will help you be incredibly successful in the position.

What are your weaknesses?

This is everyone's least favorite question. Who wants to talk about their weaknesses? Unfortunately, we have to tackle this question as it comes up often. This is the one time that you should not use the Rule of Three Technique. I would instead focus on two, rather than three weaknesses. I take this approach because I want to minimize the amount of time discussing weaknesses. Alternatively, if you only discuss one weakness, the interviewer might interpret that response as unrealistic and conclude that you're trying to avoid the question. Thus, two is the right number.

Additionally, you must demonstrate that you're self-aware and have done something to improve your weaknesses. Interviewers want to see that you're proactive about your weaknesses, which implies that you'll be proactive about your employees' short comings. Lastly, you want to be honest because it's generally obvious when you're lying.

What is the interviewer trying to understand? The interviewer wants to ascertain that your weaknesses don't disqualify you for the role. They want to understand that you have taken strides to improve your weaknesses because they want to hire problem solvers. They want to make sure you are self-aware, which implies you can effectively manage people. Lastly, they want to see how you react to a question that is very tough to answer. How do you handle pressure? How do you handle adversity?

My approach:

- Before the interview, make a list of your weaknesses and compare them to the required skills for the role. It's fine to choose weaknesses that intersect with the required skillset, but the weakness shouldn't nullify the core competencies. For example, if you're interviewing to be a project manager, don't say that you have poor organizational skills. You can, however, say that you have trouble delegating tasks, but you have improved by doing X, Y and Z.

- After completing the above step, choose two weaknesses and brainstorm what you've done to improve those weaknesses.

- Finish your answer by recognizing that everyone has weaknesses, but it's critical to improve where you can and that you have worked hard to get better.

- Keep this response brief but informative. We want to minimize the time spent answering this question.

- Be positive, forthcoming, and honest.

Example

Sure. I have two weaknesses that I've been working hard to improve.

1. First, one area I initially struggled at as a manager was delegating tasks and responsibility. As someone who is passionate about getting things done, I found myself putting too much on my plate because I was afraid to delegate work to my employees. I had this notion that they couldn't do it as well as I could. I realized, however that I, as the manager, needed to do a better

job educating and helping my direct reports. I have since scheduled one on one's on a weekly basis to provide help and feedback. I have also built joint project management tools so we have transparency into the work flow. Lastly, I have an open-door policy. Interestingly, if my direct reports don't have enough work, I have found that they will ask for more. This policy has made it easy for me to understand when things aren't working well. These tools have helped me become a more effective manager.

2. Additionally, I have historically spent too much time focusing on the current workflow and tasks at hand instead of focusing on my own personal improvement, as well as the personal development of my employees. I didn't realize that people crave information to help them get better. In order to solve this, I have set up a structure that allows for personal reflection every two weeks. When I meet with my employees, we go through their recent learnings, and then set up tools so we can put those findings to use. I have received a myriad of positive feedback from my employees on this approach. I do realize there is still plenty of room for improvement. However, I know now that focusing on your employees' personal growth is critical for having a great team of happy and productive employees.

I know everyone has weaknesses. I've been able to improve them by assessing what isn't working, and then coming up with creative solutions that I can test and iterate on.

Conclusion

There you have it! Hopefully you have found the Rule of Three Technique useful, as well as the rest of the information in this guide. If you're putting these strategies to use, I'm confident that you'll quickly see dramatic improvements as you interview more.

In the first part of this book, I provided general tips for success, as well as my five principles for improvement. In the second section, I outlined the Rule of Three Technique, how you can use it in practice, and then provided concrete examples.

If you have followed all the suggestions in this guide, you have done the following:

- Started the process of personal reflection and self-improvement, and answered questions to understand your strengths and weaknesses. This exercise forces you to use a growth mindset.

- Picked two of the interview preparation techniques and analyzed whether they worked or not.

- Written down the key players at your target company and matched them to the recruiter, hiring manager and executive. You've detailed what skills each player is looking for, and produced two examples that demonstrate the desired skillsets.

- Prepared a Situation, Action, Result response to the prompt, "Describe a situation when you used persuasion to successfully convince someone to see things your way." This exercise allows you to start practicing the Rule of Three Technique.

- Picked a company that you're interviewing with, brainstormed three reasons describing why you want to work there, and then crafted an answer using the Rule of Three Technique.

- Revised your "Walk me through your resume" using the Rule of Three Technique. This will allow you to wow in the first five minutes and can be repurposed for any interview, as long as it's tailored to the position and company.

- Created your own pitch. When used strategically, this will surprise and delight the interviewer, and differentiate you from the competition.

- Prepared a list of ten questions for your interview. You are now over prepared when it's time to ask questions.

- You've written a sample follow up email that you can then easily reference for any interview.

If you have followed all the steps in this guide, you have over prepared for your next interview. That is a great thing. By going through the process above, you have created a template to follow in any interview. This will reduce preparation time, as well as increase confidence. You will also feel less stress since you have a proven approach.

I sincerely hope that this guide has been useful. As I mentioned earlier, if you have extra time, I would be very appreciative if you wrote a review on amazon.com. If you have any questions or want to provide any feedback, please feel free to send me an email. If this book helped you get a job, I want to know about it!! So please take the time to send me a note at authoradamredding@gmail.com. Lastly, if you're an entrepreneur, small business owner, or even work in email marketing, my book "An Introduction to Email Marketing and Strategy" is great for beginners looking to learn the basics.

Good luck with your job interviewing!